A New True Book

BEARS

By Mark Rosenthal

This "true book" was prepared
under the direction of
Illa Podendorf,
formerly with the Laboratory School,
University of Chicago

 CHILDRENS PRESS, CHICAGO

Grizzly bear

PHOTO CREDITS
Mark Rosenthal—2, 8, 9 (2 photos), 11 (2 photos), 22, 30, 39, (2 photos)
James P. Rowan—4, 10, 12 (2 photos), 18, 19, 21 (left), 27, 36, 41, 44
Reinhard Brucker—Cover, 7, 16 (top), 21 (right)
Bill Thomas—15
Lynn Stone—16 (2 photos bottom), 24 (2 photos), 29, 33
Allan Roberts—35
James M. Mejuto—43
COVER—Kodiak bears

Library of Congress Cataloging in Publication Data

Rosenthal, Mark.
  Bears.

  (A New true book)
  Includes index.
  Summary: Briefly describes the different kinds of
bears, how they behave, and how they should be treated.
  1. Bears—Juvenile literature. [1. Bears.]
I. Title.
QL737.C27R67   1983   599.74′446   82-17910
ISBN 0-516-01675-X   AACR2

TABLE OF CONTENTS

Kodiak bear

WHAT IS A BEAR ?

A bear is a member of the group of animals called mammals.

Mammals are the only animals that have a body covering that we call hair. Female mammals feed their young with milk.

Bears have hair and nurse their babies with milk. Bears are mammals.

Bears are a special kind of mammal.

Scientists call the bear group carnivores. A carnivore is an animal that hunts and eats other animals. Their teeth are sharp. They can cut and tear flesh.

Sleeping Kodiak bears. Can you see their claws?

Bears also have large, strong curved claws to help them grab and hold their prey.

Polar bear

WHERE DO BEARS LIVE ?

Bears live in many places in the world.

The polar bear lives in the cold arctic regions. Its thick layer of fat and heavy fur coat protect it from the icy cold air.

Above: Asiatic black bear
Right: European brown bear

Black bears and brown bears live in North America, Europe, and Asia. These bears live in the forests and woodlands. They sleep in caves, dens, or the hollows of fallen logs.

9

Spectacled bear

The spectacled bear is the only bear that lives in South America. It lives in the mountain forests.

The spectacled bear is a small bear. It gets its name because of the hair around its eyes. This hair makes the bear look like it is wearing glasses.

Far left: The sun bear is the smallest kind of bear.
Left: Sloth bears like honey. They are sometimes called honey bears.

Sun bears and sloth bears live in the tropical forests of Asia. They are not big bears. Both are good tree climbers.

These bears spend every day asleep in a nest of branches.

Polar bears

WHAT DO BEARS EAT ?

Bears eat many kinds of food. The polar bear is a hunter. It hunts seals and other arctic animals. It is the strongest and largest hunter of the cold arctic land.

Polar bears hunt alone. Their white fur coats blend with the white snow and hide them.

When the bear sees a seal lying on the ice, it moves very slowly. It tries to hide its large body as it moves closer and closer to the seal. When it is very close to the seal, it leaps up and charges. With a little luck, it will grab the seal before it can escape into the water.

Bears at a garbage dump

Many bears will eat whatever food they can find. Brown bears and black bears go into the forest to find food. They eat plants, fruits, and insects. They also will eat small animals and the remains of dead animals.

Kodiak bears are brown bears.
They live in Alaska.

Bears have favorite foods, too.

In summer brown bears in Alaska gather in groups to catch fish swimming in streams. The brown bear will wait on shore until it sees a fish. It then leaps into the water to pin the fish to the bottom of the stream with its huge claws and mouth.

Black bear

Bears love honey.
Whenever a black bear
finds a beehive, it will eat
its fill of the sweet honey.
The stings of the angry
bees do not seem to hurt
it because of its heavy fur
coat.

Sloth bear

The sloth bear eats
insects. It uses its sharp
claws to tear apart ant
and termite nests. Then it
licks up the insects with
its tongue.

BABY BEARS

A female bear will give birth to two or three babies. They are called bear cubs. These cubs are born blind and helpless. Each cub weighs about one pound.

After about six weeks their eyes open. But they still depend on their mother for food. She will nurse them with her milk for many months.

Young black bears stay with their mothers for two years.

In springtime, the mother and cubs will come out of their den. The cubs are ready to explore their new world. They sometimes get into all kinds of trouble. There are many dangers in the forest.

Grizzly bear with cubs

The mother bear keeps
her cubs close to her. She
protects them. A mother
bear is very dangerous if
she thinks her cubs are in
trouble. She will always
help them. She will fight

other bears and enemies
to protect them.

Cubs stay with their
mother for about two
years. She shows them
how to hunt and take care
of themselves.

A mother bear may
teach her cubs to climb a
tree when in danger. The
cubs are safe high in the
tree.

Polar bear
with her cubs

24

POLAR BEARS

The polar bear is an animal that lives its life alone. The only time polar bears are together is when females and males meet during the mating season or when a female travels with her bear cubs.

Polar bear babies stay with the mother while she teaches them to hunt.

Adult bears will travel long distances to find a meal. Scientists have seen polar bears hundreds of miles from land, floating on ice floes looking for food.

A polar bear is a good hunter. It has fur on the bottom of its paws so it will not slip on the ice. It has good eyesight and a keen sense of smell.

Polar bears are strong
swimmers. They paddle
with their front feet and
steer with their back legs.

Once the Eskimos hunted the polar bear for its warm fur. It was a very dangerous hunt. An Eskimo was very brave to hunt such a powerful bear.

A large polar bear can weigh one thousand pounds and stand almost ten feet tall.

Grizzly bear

BROWN BEARS

The brown bear is the largest land meat eater in North America. It can weigh seventeen hundred pounds and stand nine feet tall.

Grizzly bears are a kind of brown bear. They weigh about eight hundred pounds.

The grizzly bear does not fear any animal. Smaller black bears will move away when a grizzly bear is near.

Grizzly bears have poor eyesight. But their senses of smell and hearing are very good.

During the summer and autumn brown bears will eat large amounts of food and grow fat. Their fur coat becomes thick.

In winter they will find a den. The den can be in a hillside or a cave. Bears live in dens during the winter months when food is hard to find.

Alaskan brown bear

Bears put grasses,
leaves, and branches into
their den. When the
weather starts to turn cold
each bear will go into its
den to sleep. Its fat and
thick coat keep it warm.

33

This sleep is not a true hibernation. The bear's body temperature does not drop very low.

A bear can wake up during the winter. It may leave its warm den for short periods of time to hunt for food.

Scientists have gone into dens looking for sleeping bears. Sometimes they have been surprised by a bear that was wide awake.

BLACK BEARS

The black bear is the most common bear in North America. It grows to a height of five feet. It can weigh three hundred pounds. It is a good tree climber.

Males and females do not travel together except during the mating season in summer.

The fur of a black bear is usually black. But sometimes the fur has a different color. It can be

Although its fur is brown, this is a black bear.

different shades of brown or yellowish to cinnamon red.

Sometimes the fur will look dirty. In summer the bear will roll in the mud and dust to get rid of biting insects.

The most famous black bear was Smokey the Bear. He was saved by forest rangers from a forest fire. He became a national symbol for fire prevention.

BEARS IN DANGER

Some bears are in danger. Without protection some bears may die.

The spectacled bear of South America is in danger. Hunters have killed too many. Others have died because the land they live on is being taken away. Farmers take the land to grow crops. When

Above: Spectacled bear cub
Left: Spectacled bear

they do, they burn the trees. They destroy the food that the bear needs to live. Then the land is good for farmers, but not for the spectacled bear.

In some places in the world it is hard for humans and bears to live close to one another. Some governments try to help the bears. They keep large areas of land free of people. They call these places national parks.

All animals in the national parks are protected. They cannot be hunted. Their land cannot be taken away.

Polar bear

Some bears like the polar bear need the help of many nations. The polar bear lives most of its life in the arctic. The countries whose land borders the arctic have agreed to protect the polar bear.

Special laws stopped people from shooting adult bears or catching bear cubs. Special places where female polar bears go to have their babies also are protected by law. These places are called wildlife reserves.

Today, in the United States, the grizzly bear is found only in national parks. The most famous place to see grizzly bears is in Yellowstone National Park.

Kodiak bear

BEARS ARE WILD ANIMALS

Bears can be dangerous.
They are very large and
powerful.

When walking in the
woods where bears are
found, a person should
sing, talk, or whistle. This

noise lets a bear know someone is near. A bear will probably run away from noise, but it can be very dangerous if surprised.

Kodiak bear

Never try to feed wild bears. When people go to a national park they sometimes see the bears begging for food. The bears seem cute and friendly. But they are not. Bears are dangerous because they can suddenly attack. Always treat bears with respect. Observe safety rules when near them.

WORDS YOU SHOULD KNOW

arctic(ARK • tick) — the part of the earth around the North Pole

carnivore(KAR • nih • vore) — an animal that feeds on the flesh of other animals; meat eater

explore(ex • PLORE) — to go into an area that is not familiar

flesh(FLESH) — the soft part of the body that covers the bones; meat

floe(FLOW) — a large, flat piece of ice floating on water

hibernate(HYE • ber • nate) — to spend the winter asleep in a protected place

keen(KEEN) — very sensitive; sharp

mammal(MAM • il) — a group of animals that have hair or fur on their bodies

predator(PRED • ah • tore) — an animal that catches and eats other animals

prey(PRAY) — an animal that is hunted or caught for food

INDEX

About the Author

Mark Rosenthal majored in Zoology at Southern Illinois University in Carbondale, Illinois. He received his Masters of Arts degree in Zoology from Northeastern Illinois State University in Chicago, Illinois. He is presently the Curator of Mammals at the Lincoln Park Zoological Gardens in Chicago.

Mark has contributed to many scientific publications including the International Zoo Yearbook, The American Association of Zoological Parks and Aquariums, The Ark (Lincoln Park Zoological Society), Primates, and The Animal Keepers Forum. The New True Book of Bears is his first publication directed to young readers. Many of Mark's photographs have appeared in other volumes in the True Book series.

DATE DUE
